FOLLOW ME

A 30-Day Walk with Jesus

FOLLOW ME

A 30-Day Walk with Jesus

DAVE RECTOR

WORDSPARK MEDIA

"Follow Me: A 30-Day Walk with Jesus"

2nd Edition

Copyright © 2020 WordSpark Media

All rights reserved Printed in the United States of America. No part of this book may be used or reproduced in any manner whatsoever without permission except in the case of brief quotations embodied in critical articles or reviews.

ISBN: Paperback (black and white interior): 978-1-7359513-2-4
Paperback (color interior): 978-1-7359513-3-1
Hardback (color interior): 978-1-7359513-4-8
eBook: 978-1-7359513-5-5

NIHIL OBSTAT
Rev. Krzysztof K. Maslowski, S.T.D.
Censor Librorum
Archdiocese of Newark
Newark, NJ, USA
August 2, 2019

IMPRIMATUR
Cardinal Joseph W. Tobin, C.Ss.R.
Archbishop of Newark
Newark, NJ, USA
August 12, 2019

The Imprimatur ("Permission to Publish") is a declaration that a book is considered to be free of doctrinal or moral error. It is not implied that those who have granted the Imprimatur agree with the contents, opinions, or statements expressed.

DEDICATION

*To my wife and best friend, Susan, who has stood beside me, always inspiring me to reach higher. I Love You Kid.
To my son, Daniel, whose sense that anything is possible both amazes and encourages me. Love You, Buddy.*

*His mother said to the servers,
"Do whatever he tells you."*
—John 2:5

CONTENTS

Foreword xi
The First—Very Unexpected—Steps xiii
Introduction xix

Your First Steps 1
Day 1   Prayer 2
Day 2   Forgiveness 7
Day 3   Helping Others 11
Day 4   Charity/Time 15
Day 5   Charity/Talent 19
Day 6   Charity/Treasure 24
Day 7   Scripture 28
Day 8   Evangelizing / Sharing the Word 31
Day 9   Loving Thy Neighbors 35
Day 10   Following the Lord 40

Further Along 43
Day 11   Prayer 44
Day 12   Forgiveness 48
Day 13   Helping Others 52
Day 14   Charity/Time 55
Day 15   Charity/Talent 59
Day 16   Charity/Treasure 63
Day 17   Scripture 65
Day 18   Evangelizing / Sharing the Word 68
Day 19   Love Thy Neighbor 72
Day 20   Following the Lord 76

For the Rest of of the Way 81
Day 21   Prayer 82
Day 22   Forgiveness 85
Day 23   Helping Others 89
Day 24   Charity/Time 93
Day 25   Charity/Talent 96
Day 26   Charity/Treasure 99
Day 27   Scripture 103
Day 28   Sharing the Word 107
Day 29   Love Thy Neighbor 110
Day 30   Following the Lord 113

Where do you go from here? Days 31–40! 117
Acknowledgements 119
About the Author 121

FOREWORD

Hearing God's invitation to help others come closer to Our Lord, Dave Rector has developed "Follow Me: A 30 Day Walk with Jesus."

I believe his reflections on scripture can help others come to a more personal encounter with Jesus through prayer, contemplation, and action.

Readers will grow in their spiritual journey, deepen their faith and, most importantly, come to live that faith each day.

Rev. Paul A. Cannariato
Pastor, Church of the Assumption
Emerson, NJ, USA

PROLOGUE
How did I get here?

THE FIRST—VERY UNEXPECTED—STEPS.

How did I get here? Or, put another way, how do I have the audacity to present the words of Jesus Christ in a program designed to change your life and help you on your way to your eternal destination?

Am I a noted clergyman? **No.**

Am I a learned Bible scholar? **Hardly.**

The holder of multiple, advanced degrees in Theology? A Deacon? A Prophet? **No, no and no.**

I was and am, quite simply, a traveler, like you.
Sometimes on a good path. Sometimes lost.
Loving the idea of following Jesus, but not always doing well.

Then, without warning, without fanfare or lightning, without the booming voice of Charlton Heston or any other theatrical effect, my life changed. Few people have heard this story until now and those that know me best might be the most surprised, even slighted, at hearing it here for the first time. My apologies.

Here is what happened, exactly as it happened. In the fall of 2011, Jesus Christ, our Savior, spoke to me. *Dramatic pause, here...* I'd like those words to hang in the air. Reread that last line: **Jesus Christ, our Savior, spoke to me**. I mean that quite literally.

I do not mean I was *inspired*. I do not mean I had a vision, or it was "as if" Jesus was talking to me. I mean, Jesus spoke to me.

I was sitting in Church, waiting for Sunday Mass to begin. I was not praying or even deep in thought. As I waited, I began to take notice of those around me. I looked from person to person, from group to group: Some sitting, others milling about. Only a few were praying. Most were involved in too-loud-for-church overlapping conversations.

None of these conversations seemed to relate to worship, the Mass or even church business. There seemed to be gossip, at least one argument and casual discussions on local sports teams and the latest scores. I shook my head and thought, quite judgmentally, "Why are they even here? They don't get it. They don't know why they are here or how to live their lives." As I said, quite judgmental on my part. At that moment I was blindsided by Jesus. He spoke: **"Why don't you tell them how to live?"**

It was not a voice from within. It was from another. Outside of me. So much so, I turned to see who was speaking.

I turned, reacting to the voice, but no one was to the right of me in the pew. No one was standing in the aisle or next to the stone wall across the aisle. No one was physically there. The voice, however, was clear.

The best way I can describe it—and this will resonate with those of a certain age—it was like the first time you heard a CD after years of listening to vinyl. The voice was clear and pure with no background noise. More so, it was calm. It was in control. Not without emotion, mind you, but without stress. Despite the challenge that was being issued, His voice was not challenging. It was pure authority, yet not without warmth or friendliness.

My reaction felt normal in the moment, but in hindsight was inexplicable. If this was a scene in a movie I should have been looking around, alarmed, frightened, even frantic - demanding to know where the voice was coming from, who was talking to me and what was going on.

I should have been looking for the closest exit! Since, however, I immediately knew who was speaking to me, I responded to the calm and the authority of the voice in as casual a way as is imaginable: I continued to look toward the blank wall at the end of the pew and engaged in conversation—my thoughts to His spoken words—as if this was an everyday occurrence. I assure you it was and is not.

We—Jesus and I—continued.

To His voiced question—"Why don't you tell them how to live?"—I responded, in thought: **"Me, tell them? How? What would I say?"**

He replied, **"Use my words."**

"Use your words?" I thought.

At that moment I could see a Bible in front of me, open to the New Testament with Jesus' words in red. These are commonly called red-letter editions of the Bible.

But I resisted: **"I'm no theologian. I don't have any authority,"** I thought.

"Tell them you do it on my authority," he said.

The assignment was clear, but I would continue to resist.

"Like I have time for this," I thought, considering the many personal and professional challenges I had at the moment. I admit this was a rather casual response considering who I was speaking to.

I heard nothing else, but sensed His smile. Almost a friendly, concluding "*I have spoken*" exclamation point on the whole exchange.

That's it. I was on my own.

Now I'd like to tell you I dropped everything—dropped my nets as Simon and Andrew did when Jesus called them to follow him. I'd like to say I abandoned all my worldly responsibilities and started living the life of an impassioned, single-minded Monk, living on bread and water and writing furiously, non-stop until my divine assignment was complete.

The truth is, I struggled. I struggled with:
- *"He's got the wrong person…"*
- *"Can I?"*
- *"How can I not?"*
- *"Should I?"*
- *"How do I?"*
- *"What will they think?"*
- *"What will they say?"*

As time went by, I also struggled with guilt. I clearly heard Jesus. I was blessed to receive divine marching orders. Yet there I was, dragging my feet.

I spoke to a few people who I trusted, in and out of the church.
I was told to proceed.
I was told to not touch it.
Once begun, I was told to abandon the whole idea.

The problem was this: It wasn't my idea, it was His. There was no escape. Unfortunately months passed, then years.

Throughout all the self-doubt, advice to quit and feeling that others would challenge my qualifications to write this book—one single line from my conversation with Jesus came back to me again and again: "Tell them you do it on my authority."

This statement also guided me each time I considered getting the approval of others. Wasn't I under His direction? Who was going to supersede that?

Despite all that, like the Biblical hero, Jonah, I had an overwhelming urge to run off, take it on the lam, and avoid my divine assignment. But I didn't run. I continued to pray, and eventually went to work, letting Him speak through me.

That's it. That's how I got here—how this 30-Day Walk came to be.
He had a reason, and the fact that this book is now in your hands is also for a reason. I pray that you find in it, that which He wants you to discover.

I pray you find the right path. A path to and with Jesus Christ.

INTRODUCTION
Mathew 4:19

"FOLLOW ME!"

Welcome and God Bless!

So, is it time to start your walk with Jesus?

Actually, the answer is "no."

The truth is, you have already been walking with Jesus. Wrapped up in your own thoughts, you most likely just didn't recognize He was there—day in and day out.

You may not have always recognized He was there, supporting you when you were trudging up hills, facing life's hardest challenges.

You may not have recognized He was there, smiling, when you crossed the finish line of each of life's races that you won—arms held high, celebrating *your own* great accomplishments. You probably didn't even recognize He was there ahead of you, directing your steps on the path to success.

But he was and is. Jesus is there at your side, right now. He patiently waits for you to notice: longing for you to notice. Unrelenting in his love, regardless of the wait.

Much of what follows will help you become more aware; recognizing and acknowledging Jesus' presence at your side. It can open you to the opportunity to know the tireless companion who already is walking along side you every moment of every day, waiting for you to accept his invitation to speak, share and ask for help: Waiting for you to follow His guidance.

The Map for Your Walk with Jesus

Each day, on this walk, you will be offered **Jesus' words**. They will appear at the top of the Day's entry.[1]

Based on His words, you will have a task—**that day's walk**—designed to bring you closer to Him.

Most of the tasks can be accomplished within a single day. Some in just minutes!

A few will take a bit longer. You don't need to finish one task before moving on. In this way, you may have days when you are working on multiple tasks. It's OK. He will be there to help you.

The tasks cover ten areas of Christian life, including Prayer, Forgiveness and Scripture. We will visit each area three times: [2]

- » From days one through ten you'll take your "First Steps" in each area.
- » Over days eleven through twenty we'll move "Further Along".
- » Finally, during days twenty-one through thirty we will focus on making each area a part of your daily life "For the Rest of the Way."

---

[1] All Gospel quotations have been drawn from United States Conference of Catholic Bishops website.
[2] I believe it is worth noting that this structure was not planned by me, it was revealed as I accepted my assignment and began work.

	DISCIPLINE	FIRST STEPS	FURTHER ALONG	FOR THE REST OF THE WAY
1	Prayer	Day 1	Day 11	Day 21
2	Forgiveness	Day 2	Day 12	Day 22
3	Helping Others	Day 3	Day 13	Day 23
4	Charity: Time	Day 4	Day 14	Day 24
5	Charity: Talent	Day 5	Day 15	Day 25
6	Charity: Treasure	Day 6	Day 16	Day 26
7	Scripture	Day 7	Day 17	Day 27
8	Sharing the Word	Day 8	Day 18	Day 28
9	Love thy Neighbor	Day 9	Day 19	Day 29
10	Following the Lord	Day 10	Day 20	Day 30

Each day, you will get examples and ideas, but it is **up to you** to apply the task to your life and specific situation.

You will be asked to write down your experiences, thoughts and challenges in your **Personal Journal**. This is for you and will prove valuable as you move forward, each day. Later, it will help should you return to an unfinished item. Still later, it will help you review where you were, where you went and how you felt.

Three important points:

1. This program is not intended to be simply read. Reading or skimming through the daily walks offers little inspiration and will have little to no affect: **The glory is in the doing.** The result is dependent on what you actually do during and through each task. That is how you will connect with Jesus.

2. This program is not meant to be kept in pristine condition, sitting on a shelf. As you read the book, underline freely, dog ear pages, fill the

margin with notes. If using an electronic version, make separate notes as you go down the path. And, most importantly, make entries in your Personal Journal.

3. This part of your life-long journey, this short walk, is slated for 30 days. That is ideal, but by no means required. Miss a day or take a bit longer with a task? That's OK: Forgiveness is served in generous portions here. Stumbling and righting yourself are all part of the plan: His plan…and His acceptance of each of us.

You and I are works in progress. They'll be some rerouting along the way, but the greatest Guide of all time is here to help—if you are ready. Let's recognize Him and get the most from this journey.

DAYS 1–10

Jesus Helps with Your First Steps

Day 1

FIRST STEPS: PRAYER

Luke 11:1-4
He was praying in a certain place, and when he had finished, one of his disciples said to him, "Lord, teach us to pray just as John taught his disciples." He said to them, *"When you pray, say: Father, hallowed be your name, your kingdom come. Give us each day our daily bread and forgive us our sins for we ourselves forgive everyone in debt to us, and do not subject us to the final test."*

Today, Jesus, Once Again, Teaches Us to Pray

I remember that "Wow moment" as a child watching the 1956 version of "King of Kings," rerun as it usually was in the '70s on TV during Easter Week. A follower calls out "Rabbi, teach us to pray." Jesus replies with The Lord's Prayer.

"Wait," I thought. "*The Lord's Prayer... The Our Father...* That's direct from Jesus? Really? They didn't make that up in Sunday school? Wow!"

When you think about it, this is as good as it gets. An amazing opportunity to pray in the words Jesus himself gave us. I think it is profoundly revealing that in so few words Jesus gave us all that we need: a clear, concise prayer covering every essential aspect of our daily lives.

Truly, its strength is in its simplicity: The right way to live each day, boiled down to a few indispensable lines.

Listen as Never Before
Consistent with that simplicity, this first day of your 30-Day Walk with Jesus, will be simple.

Simple, yet profound—if, you truly open your mind and heart.

All you need do is pray the Lord's Prayer—but you need to listen, perhaps as you never have before.

First, prepare yourself. Find a place to pray. Truly you can pray anywhere, but it may be helpful to locate a spot where you can find calm and peace—a place you can return to again and again. Perhaps it is a room in your home, your yard or a nearby park. Make sure it is accessible, comfortable—and reasonably quiet.

Begin to pray. You can use either the version of Our Lord's Prayer found in Luke as shown above or the one found in Matthew 6:9-13. You can also use what, for many, may be a more familiar version found in the Catechism of the Catholic Church (2759), and shown below.

Begin to pray. Slowly. Contemplate each line.

Our Father who art in heaven, hallowed be thy name.
>Jesus tells you to call on the Father, giving Him praise by acknowledging his holiness.

Thy kingdom come. Thy will be done on earth as it is in heaven.
>As his kingdom is established on earth—which happens every day, through each of us, His will shall be obeyed by all, as it is in heaven. We give ourselves up to His authority. The benefits of being obedient to His will are innumerable, profound, and glorious.

Give us this day our daily bread,
>Lord, I pray—and trust—that You will give me what I need today, mentally, physically and spiritually.

and forgive us our trespasses,
>Lord, show me forgiveness—release me from the debt of my sins.

as we forgive those who trespass against us,
>And, by Your grace, Lord, let me follow Your example and forgive those who may have wronged me in things big and small.

and lead us not into temptation, but deliver us from evil.
>Protect us from the temptations of Satan who works to separate us from God.

Personal Journal
What did you think of today's first steps on your walk?

As you prayed, did you experience "The Lord's Prayer" anew?

Did anything surprise you? A word or phrase resonating as it hadn't before? Clarity? A new perspective?

A Step Further: Sharing Today's Walk

Who should you tell about your walk with Christ today? Who would benefit from hearing your story? Go ahead. Tell them.

Journal your experience in sharing.

Day 2

FIRST STEPS: FORGIVENESS

Mathew 6:14
If you forgive others their transgressions, your heavenly Father will forgive you.

Today, Jesus Teaches Us to Forgive

Today, staying with the spirit of The Lord's Prayer, we want to cast a wide net in terms of forgiveness. Let Jesus give you the gift of peace by letting go of some negative things in your heart.

Start by thinking of anyone you have an issue with, big or small. Don't try to resolve any of the situations immediately and don't get yourself worked up reliving each issue.

Simply write down the person's name and a short, few word description of what you feel the trespass was. Hopefully it is a short list, but however long it is, so be it.

We Forgive Those Who Trespass Against Us
Now, go back to the top. Put all animosity aside. Read the person's name. Picture them in your mind. Pray for an open heart to release your grievance against them: forgive them their trespass. Take as much time as you need to pray—but again, do not relive the offense. Ask for His help. Listen in silence for guidance or perhaps just a feeling of peace. Picture the person again. Stop and smile. Then draw a line through just their trespass—not their name.

Continue down the list, slowly repeating this pattern for each name on the list.

At the end, you will have a list of names. People who you can release and forgive. And depending on the relationships, a list of people who today you can start with anew. Next time you see each person or hear from them, hopefully it will be with a light and open heart.

Personal Journal
Were you able to avoid getting worked up, focusing on forgiveness and not the offense?

_____

_____

_____

_____

If you felt agitated, did you pray for calm? Why or why not?

_____
_____
_____
_____

A Step Further: Sharing Today's Walk
Do you know someone who is holding a grudge, large or small? List them below.

_____
_____
_____
_____

Would it help them to learn about today's walk and how they might apply it? Why or why not?

_____
_____
_____
_____

Why not share it with them? If you do, describe your experience here.

Day 3

FIRST STEPS: HELPING OTHERS

John 13:34-35
I give you a new commandment: love one another. As I have loved you, so you also should love one another. This is how all will know that you are my disciples, if you have love for one another."

Today, Jesus Teaches Us to Help Someone in Need

I always liked the iconic image of the charitable organization Boy's Town: An older boy carrying a younger one on his back and responding to a question from, Boy's Town founder, Father Flanagan as to whether the younger boy was too heavy to be carried. The answer of course is: "He ain't heavy, Father, he's my brother."

When we are doing for others with an open heart, nothing seems too much of a burden—no one is too heavy to carry. Of course, since we are all children of God, every person is your brother or sister.

In John 13:34-35, Jesus commands his disciples to follow his example and love each other as he has loved them. Bear in mind with this command Jesus significantly raised the bar: From that time forward the instruction changed from "love your neighbor as yourself" to "As I have loved you, so you also should love one another." Remember as He loved us was to the level of laying down his life for us! Today, we can start to love one another as Jesus has loved us in a small way by extending a helping hand—by carrying someone when they need it. Today, let's start with someone close—a family member or close friend.

Extend a Helping Hand

Is there someone struggling with a problem who could use a sympathetic, undistracted ear?
Is advice needed?
Could a few dollars make all the difference to them?
Is someone's "To Do" list overwhelming them? Could you take a task off them to lighten their burden—help carry them by giving them a little less to carry?
It doesn't have to be big. Today, just do something to help—and do it with an open heart.
Love them as Jesus loves you. Willingly sacrifice, just a bit of your time, attention, or resources.

Personal Journal

Describe your experience helping someone today.

_____

_____

_____

Did more than one person come to mind when you were thinking of those who needed help? How did you choose who to help?

_____

_____

_____

_____

Could you continue helping others on your list in the coming days?

_____

_____

_____

_____

Do you see how this could become a habit?

_____

_____

_____

_____

14 | FOLLOW ME: A 30-DAY WALK WITH JESUS

Why stop?

_____

_____

_____

_____

_____

_____

_____

A Step Further: Sharing Today's Walk
Today you helped with something small but important. If the next time you help the task is larger you might need to engage a friend—a two-person job—done on behalf of someone. Think how much that friend might get out of helping you help someone else.

Day 4

FIRST STEPS: CHARITY/TIME

Luke 6:31

"Treat men exactly as you would like them to treat you."

Today, Jesus Teaches Us to Give of Our Time

It is likely you have often heard of charitable giving being broken down into three categories: Time, Talent and Treasure. We will do the same on our journey. Today, we will start with Time.

What a simple idea Jesus offers us for today's walk: "Treat men exactly as you would like them to treat you." This and Mathew 7:12, are the roots of what is commonly called the Golden Rule.

While simple in concept, the real-world challenge here is in the effort. You know how you would like others to treat you, but sometimes returning the favor requires effort—effort we are not always inclined to put forth.

Like many of us, from time to time I will get frustrated with work and career. I sometimes wish someone would just listen to me. I may not even need advice: just let me get it off my chest and I'll be fine. Often, I find a willing, charitable soul in the person of my wife or my son, and I am grateful for their time. But when the tables are turned, sometimes minutes later, and that same person who was willing to listen to me needs a few minutes of my time, it's a different story. I find myself short on patience. I wanted to be listened to, but I'll stare at the same charitable soul—who took time for me—expressing their own frustrations, and what do I do? I start tapping my foot or nodding quickly trying to move them along. I think: "Okay, Okay, get on with it. We're just wasting time with your whining. I don't have time to listen to you!"

I'm not treating them exactly as I wanted them to treat me.
I'm not treating them exactly as they **did** treat me.
I am not being charitable with my time.

Choose One Person to Help

So today, in the context of treating others as you would want to be treated, your path is to be charitable with your time, just as you would like others to be:

- » Perhaps someone needs your time to listen to a problem.
- » Time to run an errand.
- » Is there an older neighbor who would appreciate you picking something up from the store?
- » Do you have co-workers putting in extra hours, who might appreciate a coffee run?
- » Is someone sick that could have their whole day turned around by a half-hour visit—just letting them know someone cares?

Just look at your family members, friends, neighbors, co-workers.

Put yourself in their position, whatever that position is, and ask yourself:

"How would I like to be treated?"—then act by choosing one person and giving them your **time** today.

Personal Journal

How much time did it actually take to be charitable today?

What was the reaction of the person you helped?

How did it make you feel?

_____

_____

_____

_____

_____

_____

_____

A Step Further: Sharing Today's Walk
This simple concept is easy to emulate in small and large ways. We just need a reminder from time to time. If you reminded your friends about treating others as they would want to be treated and gave them the example of how you shared your time, do you think they would be encouraged to do something similar?

Day 5

FIRST STEPS: CHARITY/TALENT

Mathew 25:14-30
"It will be as when a man who was going on a journey called in his servants and entrusted his possessions to them. To one he gave five talents; to another, two; to a third, one—to each according to his ability. Then he went away. Immediately the one who received five talents went and traded with them, and made another five. Likewise, the one who received two made another two. But the man who received one went off and dug a hole in the ground and buried his master's money. After a long time the master of those servants came back and settled accounts with them. The one who had received five talents came forward bringing the additional five. He said, 'Master, you gave me five talents. See, I have made five more. His master said to him, 'Well done, my good and faithful servant. Since you were faithful in small matters, I will give you great responsibilities. Come, share your master's joy.' [Then] the one who had received two talents also came forward and said, 'Master,

you gave me two talents. See, I have made two more.' His master said to him, 'Well done, my good and faithful servant. Since you were faithful in small matters, I will give you great responsibilities. Come, share your master's joy.' Then the one who had received the one talent came forward and said, 'Master, I knew you were a demanding person, harvesting where you did not plant and gathering where you did not scatter; so out of fear I went off and buried your talent in the ground. Here it is back.' His master said to him in reply, 'You wicked, lazy servant! So you knew that I harvest where I did not plant and gather where I did not scatter? Should you not then have put my money in the bank so that I could have got it back with interest on my return? Now then! Take the talent from him and give it to the one with ten. For to everyone who has, more will be given and he will grow rich; but from the one who has not, even what he has will be taken away. And throw this useless servant into the darkness outside, where there will be wailing and grinding of teeth.'

Today, Jesus Teaches Us to Use Our Talents to Help Others

One of my favorite non-bible quotes is:
"If you have a talent, that's God's gift to you; If you use it, that's your gift to God."

Another, closely related, is:
"To give anything less than your best is to sacrifice the gift."

To remind myself of these ideas, I have these two quotes (along with Romans 8:31 and others) permanently fixed at the top of my daily Action Plan on my computer.

In today's parable, although the media is ancient money (Talents) the idea is how you are using that which you have been given, your unique gifts, to honor the Lord. In fact, the English word Talent comes down to us from this parable.

Those that use their talents honor the Lord and are entrusted with more. I remember being confused when I first studied this parable. The servant that buried the money that was entrusted to him did not commit an aggressive or egregious transgression: he didn't steal the money. He didn't spend it on partying and drinking or anything else. He feared failure and so did nothing with his talents—those gifts entrusted to him. After a while, it became clear to me: doing nothing was the problem. He was sacrificing the gift. His gift. His talent.

Are you burying your talent? Talents are alive, with energy and potential—use them and they create more! More excitement! More activity! More participation! When your talents are used to further the Father's work that is, simply put, a very good thing. And when your talents are attributed back to the Father people appreciate it and can also look at their own God-given talents—and just may be motivated to put them to work.

So let's not bury our talent.

Now, my one quibble with the first non-bible quote I mentioned above is the first few words "if you have a talent..." We ALL have God-given talents. You may be a gifted painter. An excellent writer. An incomparable organizer. A great runner. A remarkable baker. You may be an outstanding App developer or a programmer. You may be good at making phone calls—sales, soliciting volunteers, raising awareness for a cause. You may be a wonderful listener. I know one person whose talent is the ability to make people feel good—even people she doesn't know. They meet her on an elevator, talk and by the end of the ride they feel better—remarkable. Are you generous? Generosity itself is a talent—the willingness to give unselfishly. The list of possibilities is endless.

Start with a List and Create a Plan

Today, return to that blank page or screen and start listing your talents.

What has God given you, that should not be buried? What has He given you that should be invested (used) to create interest: To honor the Lord, bring joy, or affect people's lives?

Not all talents are big and loud or out in front. Some work effectively in the background.

Be honest. Spend no more than 10 minutes and list your talents.

Now, take no more than 5 SECONDS for this next step; Look at your list and immediately—almost without thinking—Circle one item on the list. Trust yourself in doing this.

Congratulations, you just gave yourself your marching orders! Today, let's put this talent—the one you circled—to work for your family, your community, your church—and ultimately for the Lord.

Organizers can organize an awareness campaign or fundraiser. Listeners can extend themselves to those in need. Painters and writers can start a new project. Teachers and Coaches can expand their program or focus their attention on a specific student or athlete in need. You get the idea.

You may finish this task in one day—or, the work you start here may have you using your talents for weeks, month or longer. Today, however, you will identify and plan how to use your talent—and you will get STARTED!

Personal Journal
Did you have trouble listing your talents? Why do you think that is?

_____

_____

_____

_____

Once done, did you feel better?

_____

_____

_____

_____

Do you have a new appreciation for the Talents God has given you? How does this make you feel?

_____

_____

_____

_____

A Step Further: Sharing Today's Walk

Once you are beyond your list and actually start using your talents, people will see what you are doing so no need to go out of your way to share the "What"—but, make sure to share the "Why".

Day 6

FIRST STEPS: CHARITY/TREASURE

Mark 12:43-44
Calling his disciples to himself, he said to them, "Amen, I say to you, this poor widow put in more than all the other contributors to the treasury. For they have all contributed from their surplus wealth, but she, from her poverty, has contributed all she had, her whole livelihood."

Today, Jesus Teaches Us to Give More

For many of us, the general act of being charitable with our treasure has been ingrained in us from an early age. In church there are collections and fundraisers and various efforts to help the poor or those temporarily in need. Outside of church, TV commercials, billboards, ads and social media campaigns ask us to give to various causes and in doing so we feel good. "I did my part." or "At least I did something." Even: "it's the least I can do." Do these contributions help the mission or organization they are intended for? If it is an honest, and well-run organization, the likely answer is 'yes': every bit helps. But is that what Jesus asks us to do: give a bit? Give a little? In the story of the poor widow, the reality of the amount is brought up. While the poor widow gives less in total compared to the wealthy contributors that precede and follow her, the percentage she gives is much more than theirs. They are giving from their abundance, she is giving from her want.

So today, we will be like the poor widow that Jesus held up as an example. Today, we will give, not just from our surplus. There is no swapping here; You can't say I can't afford it, so I will give my time or talent. Those are charitable acts for other days on this walk. You know what your limits are. We are not suggesting you give all you have—but can you give a little more than you think?

Challenge Yourself

1. Consider a recent contribution you have made to your church, the poor or a favorite charitable organization. Or maybe just a contribution you were considering. Write down the amount of the contribution.

2. Take a breath. Look away from the paper. Look out at the sky, nature, a bird, your children, your parents, God's handiwork is all around us. Nothing nearby? Consider the day and thank the Lord for it. Say a little prayer.

3. Now go back to the paper—or the screen—and take another look at the amount of your contribution. Can you increase it? Can you commit to doing that—even if it is inconvenient?

4. Write down a new figure. Do it now.

5. Turn away again. Take another deep breath. Now, go back. Cross out the second amount and write down a new one. Can you commit to this new amount? More so, can you actually make that contribution today?

For some the third figure may be just a few dollars more than the first. For others it may be a bit higher. It truly is not the amount that is important. What is important is the act of emulating the poor widow. The one Jesus choose to hold up to his disciples as an example. The one he willed to be remembered through scripture, specifically so her example could be given to us—to you—this very day.

Personal Journal
Were you surprised at the 3rd amount you wrote down?

_____

_____

_____

Did it frighten you when you had considered the final amount? Did you feel you might be leaving yourself too short for your needs? Remember our mission is to store up treasure in heaven.

_____

_____

_____

Did you feel guilty that the final amount was not enough? Remember it is not the amount but the idea of truly giving.

_____

How did you feel when you actually made the donation?

Come back to this question when the time is right: Did I receive back—in one way or another—more than I gave?

A Step Further: Sharing Today's Walk
Being careful not to brag or complain, share the joy that giving has brought you and thereby encourage others.

Day 7

FIRST STEPS: SCRIPTURE

Mathew 4:4
He said in reply, *"It is written: 'One does not live by bread alone, but by every word that comes forth from the mouth of God.'"*

Today, Jesus Teaches Us to Trust in Scripture

In a society and a culture that does not read unless text is reduced to bullet points, where complex news stories and issues are reduced to 10-second sound bites, how formidable and how alien the thousands of pages of the Bible seem to most of us. Those of us who are so called "avid" readers almost always are challenged with our own reading lists—personal and professional—that never seem to grow smaller. Plus, the reasons not to read the Bible are readily available: *The Bible is too long; the language is too complex or out of date; It is too confusing; It is not relevant.*

Take a Leap of Faith

On today's path with Jesus, your joyful task is not to start reading the Bible from cover to cover. Take a Bible in your hand—hopefully you do have one. If not, perhaps you can bring up an online version. Consider it. What you are holding in your hand—or looking at on-screen, is the Word of God! Now, with that thought in mind and confident in his direction for your life, take a leap of faith: a leap straight into the pages of the Bible. The starting point is entirely up to you. Start at the beginning, seek out a favorite book of the Bible, or a favorite story. Simply open the Bible and read. Read a single verse, a few verses, read a number of pages. Flip around. Try to come away with something that interests or touches you.

If you find something that you can apply in your day-to-day life or to a specific situation—do so. Or pass on the thought to someone else who it could help. The opportunity to use an idea from what you have read may not present itself today, but at some point, it will. Remember today's task is just to take the leap, open His Word and read something.

Personal Journal

Write down the Book of the Bible, Chapter and Verses that you read in your Personal Journal below. Make a few notes about what you understood from your reading; what you got out of it, that you can use. Write down any questions you have.

Note that you might use a portion of these notes on Day 13.

A Step Further: Sharing Today's Walk
Since you are just taking your first steps here, a simple comment such as, "I started reading the Bible today" might be compelling enough to start a conversation and inspire others. Why not try?

Day 8

FIRST STEPS: EVANGELIZING / SHARING THE WORD

Matthew 10:32
Everyone who acknowledges me before others I will acknowledge before my heavenly Father.

Today, Jesus Teaches Us to Confess Him Before Men

I have travelled extensively, working with groups of salespeople visiting cities for tradeshows. These men were excellent at their *profession*, yet, not what you might describe as *professional*: They weren't polished, disciplined or well behaved—they were not choirboys. They were rough, loud, confident—maybe over-confident. They were not opposed to getting into some trouble, either of their own making or trouble they came upon. It was not unlikely, before any given night was over, one or more of them would be in a street or bar altercation, or worse. Over the years I became adept at talking bouncers out of acting, negotiating instead for five extra minutes to lead our group out of their establishment.

A gathering of this aggressive, Type A, alpha-male-laden group did not seem like the ideal place for a heartfelt discussion of God's impact on our lives. I certainly would not have been compelled to raise the subject. It seemed likely to fall on deaf ears, be laughed off and cast aside. So, sadly, I never tried.

One night, however, I got a masters-level course in what's possible—what He can do. I don't know who brought up Jesus, but someone did and once it was on the table I sat back, amazed and gratified as one by one these irreverent, tough guys talked—confidently—about what God had done for them. Getting them through addiction, marital issues, children's illnesses; business problems, loss of parents, and worse. No they weren't choirboys. Not reverent in the traditional sense—each, very much a work in progress—but as they talked and shared, I felt each was heartened by the other's stories. As each confessed Christ, the others were both open to sharing their own faith and more encouraged to let Jesus play a greater role.

Sometimes it only takes the courage of one, in the most unlikely of circumstances to open doors, minds and hearts.

Start with One Person
Now I'll admit speaking in or to groups can be intimidating. Today, let's start slowly. Start by listing your blessings. For some the list will be long. If you are blessed that much, limit your list to the top five. If you can think of just one, that's OK. Go with that one (and trust me, your list will get longer).

Now, think of one person to share this with. That one person may be someone you are comfortable speaking to. Or, it may be someone who you know needs to be reminded of Jesus' love. Perhaps it's someone that doesn't know Jesus at all.

Reach out—call, email, stop by or meet—and tell that person how Jesus' love has—and is—affecting you. That's all you need to do. He'll take it from there.

Personal Journal
How did you feel when you finished your list of blessings?

_____

_____

_____

_____

_____

_____

Was it difficult coming up with a person to share with? Why or why not?

_____

_____

_____

_____

When you shared, did the conversation take any unexpected turns? What were they? Why do you think that happened?

A Step Further: Sharing Today's Walk
Speaking with a friend or family member—or even a casual acquaintance—about today's walk can't help but get them thinking about their own blessings. What a blessed gift to give them!

Day 9

FIRST STEPS: LOVING THY NEIGHBORS

Matthew 22:39
The second is like it: You shall love your neighbor as yourself.

Today, Jesus Teaches Us to Love Our Neighbor

Love your neighbor as yourself. We are often eager to follow these words. Perhaps, because we see so many benefits for ourselves. If we define our neighbors as not only those who live in proximity but those whose circles we travel in: Other church members, co-workers, the den mother of your child's scout troop, the guy on the next bar stool… whoever it is, there are benefits to engaging with these people, doing them favors, looking out for them, helping them out. It often benefits us. At the very least, it reflects back on us positively in our varied communities and groups. But, is that the idea? I think to truly love your neighbor, to see to their needs and make sure they are right with God, you must *know* them. Oops! It just got a little more difficult, didn't it?

There was a man I saw in my neighborhood for years. His behavior was, let's say somewhat odd in my opinion. his attire was not what anyone would expect, often dressing remarkably out of season: Shorts and sandals in January in the Northeast! Largely, I ignored him. Later I came to find out he was a leading expert in a particular field: not the field he worked in, but another entirely unrelated field that he dedicated himself to in his off hours. For many years, aside from being put off by his odd style of dress, I could not have loved him because I knew nothing of him. Later when I came to know him, I was able to discuss his interests and learn from him. This gratified him and satisfied his need to teach. I'd wish him well before he went off to conferences and lectures. We became friends.

First, You Have to Know Your Neighbor

Today as a first step to loving your neighbor, pick out someone you come in contact with on a regular basis, but do not truly know.

It could be a co-worker, an acquaintance, someone you pass on the street every day, a club member who always sits on the opposite side of the room.

Make an effort to learn more about this person—your neighbor. See what you can learn. Be careful. Unfortunately, in today's world coming on too strong with questions can raise suspicions and defensive walls. One or two friendly questions to start a conversation will do. Remember you will likely have to share a bit about yourself to make sure it is a conversation—not an interrogation.

If you uncover a need that you can help with, do so. If what you learn is just that you will speak with this neighbor again, be happy with that. *All glory comes from daring to begin*[3]: Dare to *know* your neighbor, so that you can start to *love* your neighbor.

---

3   Eugene F. Ware

Personal Journal

Did picking a "neighbor" to get to know better frighten you? Why do you think that is?

_____

_____

_____

_____

Once you reached out did you learn anything surprising about your neighbor? About yourself?

_____

_____

_____

_____

Can you take what you learned and use it to approach others in the future?

_____

_____

_____

_____

A Step Further: Sharing Today's Walk

What motivated you to pick the person you decided to get to know?

_____

_____

_____

_____

Did choosing this particular person benefit you in any way? How?

_____

_____

_____

_____

Were you surprised about what you learned about "your neighbor?"

_____

_____

_____

_____

_____

_____

How might today's walk change your view of your other neighbors?

Day 10

FIRST STEPS: FOLLOWING THE LORD

Luke 10:41-42
The Lord said to her in reply, *"Martha, Martha, you are anxious and worried about many things. There is need of only one thing. Mary has chosen the better part and it will not be taken from her."*

Today, Jesus Teaches Us the Importance of Spending Time with Him

How backwards this story seems to us. Martha is running about doing all the work preparing the dinner and Mary is sitting, lounging if you will, and spending time with Jesus. Martha complains and asks that Mary be forced to do her fair share. And we think: "Yeah, that's right, it's only fair! Here it comes… Mary's about to be blasted for her inconsiderate ways—letting Martha do all the work? And then Jesus flips things around and shows us another side, as only he can. *Martha, Martha, you are anxious and worried about many things. There is need of only one thing. Mary has chosen the better part and it will not be taken from her."* Wait! Hold on! In this multi-tasking, work-around-the-clock, never-disconnected, 24-hour email and texting world we live in, we are supposed to believe that Martha—the one we likely identify with the most—the one running about and chipping away at her To Do list is, in fact, wrong? According to Jesus? *Yup. Sorry.*

You can give a higher priority to all your tasks, and assignments. All your To Do list items. Everything our culture tells you to focus on, and you will have missed the only item that truly matters: Spending time with Jesus. In His presence. In His house. In His Word. In His Spirit.

Update Your To Do List
Today's task is oh so simple. You will make a new entry in your To Do list. However and wherever you keep it... on the refrigerator... on your computer... in your tablet or smart phone... you will make one entry PERMANENT and keep it at the top of the list: **Spend Time with Jesus**. In quiet prayer. In Mass. On a long walk. And today you will do that before all other things. And tonight or tomorrow, when it's time to update that list, remember, this is one part of your To Do list that you will not check off, delete, edit or alter.

Personal Journal
Can you commit to spending time with Jesus today?

Can you do it every day?

How will you spend time with Jesus? Praying? Going to Mass? Evangelizing? Doing for others? Note your plan below.

A Step Further: Sharing Today's Walk
Remember in trying to share, a simple, compelling statement can start an interesting conversation with profound impact. Consider: "I was spending time with Jesus today..."

DAYS 11–20

Jesus Guides Us Further Along

Day 11

FURTHER ALONG: PRAYER

Mark 11:24
Therefore I tell you, all that you ask for in prayer, believe that you will receive it and it shall be yours.

Today, Jesus Teaches Us to Pray, with Faith, That He Will Do What is Best for Us

When speaking with someone who is skeptical about Jesus, I calmly offer a standard challenge: Spend a week with me, in prayer, and see if prayer doesn't change your life.

How can I be so confident in this challenge? Because I have seen the power of prayer firsthand. I know that real, consistent, devout prayer can be startling, surprising, eye-opening, and truly amazing. Once you have experienced the life-changing effect of prayer, you cannot deny its power and the fact that God is at work in our lives—we just need to invite him in.

Let me explain. At perhaps the lowest point in my life, I was at a loss what to do next. I was in a bad financial situation and saw no possible way out. I turned to prayer. Honestly, I did so with no real hope it would work. I turned to prayer out of desperation like George Baily on the bridge in "It's A Wonderful Life."

But I did pray. Devoutly. Consistently and with complete surrender: "Lord I can't fix this. I don't think it can be fixed, but if it can, I have to leave it to you."

Now you may not think that is an appropriate way to pray, and I certainly wasn't at a stage in my journey where I understood the idea of total surrender, but, I was inadvertently practicing what is in fact a powerful act of faith (although that was not my intention).

You don't need to understand how things will work out, as much as you need to accept that He will do what's best for you. And while my approach was slightly off center in that I was surrendering, but not confidently, not out of faith, it was nevertheless sincere. "Jesus help me. I need your help. I'm in your hands."

As I said, I also prayed consistently. Multiple times of day. And my life began to change. To my former way of thinking it was inexplicable. As illogical as it seemed to me at the time, things changed—my life changed. He took the burden. To me this confirmed the power of prayer and, more importantly, the power of prayer has proven itself time and time again since then. I look back on that first time I surrendered and think how much easier it would have been if I had surrendered with confidence—with complete faith.

Lack of faith is akin to worry, and worry is a sin. Most of us see sin as an outward act: stealing, hating, or hurting someone. Worry, however, is inward, so how, you may ask, could it be a sin if you are only hurting yourself? First, the Lord doesn't want you to be hurt, even by your own act, and second, to worry is to doubt him.

Pray BIG

So today, you will not only pray faithfully but you will go an extra step and pray BIG! Return to the prayer place you selected on Day 1 of this journey; the place you have hopefully visited every day since we started. Praying BIG means not limiting your prayers. Do not apply your own logic of what is and is not possible—pray BIG, and with complete faith: "...*believe that you will receive it and it shall be yours.*"

The answer may not be exact. It may not be immediate: remember it will be in His time, not yours. But, in the long run, you will discover the answer will be what you truly need.

Personal Journal

Did you approach today's challenge with an open mind, or were you skeptical about praying BIG?

_____

_____

_____

_____

How can you be more open minded?

_____

_____

_____

Did you truly pray BIG or were you still being conservative?

A Step Further: Sharing Today's Walk
We share our hopes and dreams frequently. Just as easily, we can share our prayers. Just tell anyone you choose what you are praying for. Those who you share your prayers with might start praying for their own BIG desires. That would be a very good thing. They might even pray that your prayers are fulfilled. That would also be a very good thing. They might do both. That would be awesome!

Day 12

FURTHER ALONG: FORGIVENESS

Mathew 5:9
Blessed are the peacemakers, for they will be called children of God.

Today, Jesus Teaches Us to Live Forgiveness

On Day 2 we asked you to make a list of people who you had felt trespassed against you and to forgive them in your heart: To let it go. Today we want to take a more active approach.

Jesus' message is so simple and clear: *"Blessed are the Peacemakers..."*—And the payoff is so big: *"for they will be called children of God."* To be called children of God... think of all that goes with that: peace, ultimate happiness, a place with God, all the angels and the saints in heaven for all eternity. How could anything or anyone stop us from such a clear path? Ah, but, something and someone does stop us: Our fears and ourselves. Our earthly thoughts get in our way, and we stop ourselves cold.

Let's face it: To be a peacemaker requires risk. As a third party interjecting yourself as a mediator into an argument between co-workers, you risk having your involvement and motives questioned and your solutions rejected by one or both sides. A similar act, mediating between family members, is the same with the bigger risk of alienating loved ones. If you are a combatant—part of the argument, disagreement, or battle—peacemaking runs the risk of being seen as weak, losing or giving in. Or, again, having your solution or olive branch rejected. But is it worth the risk: First, potentially ending a conflict, and then to be counted as being among the children of God? Yes, *I'd say it is worth any risk.*

Be the Beginning of the End

Later in this journey we can attack big problems, even work to save the world, but today let's start smaller and closer to home: Not that this won't be a challenge, mind you!

Is there a dispute that you are part of?
Stop. Think about it.
Is there a disagreement at work?
With a neighbor?
With a family member?
Perhaps it is a long-standing grudge with your brother.
An unresolved disagreement with one of your kids or a parent.
Most of us have something that needs to be addressed.

Today is the day.
Step into that person's office. Go next door or pick up the phone.
Don't text or email, unless it's to ask for time to talk. You need to do this personally, whether it's face-to-face or over the phone.
Take the risk.

In many battles you don't even have to declare a winner or lay blame:
- » "Susan, I'm sorry."
- » "Bob, I'd like to put this behind us."
- » "Evalyn, we're sisters and we shouldn't let this come between us."

Many times the risk—what we fear—is just that—a fear. Unfounded.

One that will go up in smoke as soon as you step up and face it.

I'm not saying you won't get push back. I'm not saying everything will go smoothly or there is no chance that there will be more hurt feelings or old wounds reopened. What I am saying is if someone doesn't take the first step, reach out and offer a solution, it may never get done. Why not be the peacemaker? Why not be counted among the children of God?

Personal Journal
Were you nervous before you reached out?

_____

_____

_____

Did you truly try to be a peacemaker rather than just trying to circle back, re-engage and win the battle?

_____

_____

_____

Did you do the best you could? Listening more than talking?

What was the result?

A Step Further: Sharing Today's Walk
Could your story inspire others to do the same in their lives? Who could you help by sharing today's progress?

Day 13

FURTHER ALONG: HELPING OTHERS

Mark 16:15
He said to them, *"Go into the whole world and proclaim the gospel to every creature."*

Today, Jesus Teaches Us to Help Others with His Word

On Day 3 you had the choice to help someone close to you in whatever way they needed at the moment. This was somewhat of a wide-open opportunity: There are so many ways to help someone. Today we will add a little focus and follow Jesus' teaching to help in a very specific way. Today we will help by sharing the gospel.

Share Something that Touches Your Heart

Now we aren't going to ask you to become a bible scholar in one day or be prepared to debate scripture with others. All we want you to do is share something that touches your heart.

Start with your favorite Bible verse. Why does this verse speak to you? Think about it. Would sharing that verse and how or why it touches you be somewhat of a challenge? That's okay. Jesus is with you, and, with Him, you are up to the challenge of today's walk.

Share this verse and the reason it touches you with as many people as you can today. As many people as you can: There is no quota. One is good. Two is better, three is great. No matter how many people you reach, what greater way to help people than to give then a path to salvation?

Personal Journal

Did you have trouble picking a verse to share? Why?

_____

_____

_____

_____

_____

_____

_____

Were you nervous or confident? If nervous, would it have helped to think of Jesus being with you?

A Step Further: Sharing Today's Walk
As noted above, a key part of today's task is to share, so have at it!

Day 14

FURTHER ALONG: CHARITY/TIME

Luke 10:2-12
He said to them, "The harvest is abundant but the laborers are few; pray therefore the Lord of the Harvest to send out laborers into his harvest. Go your way; behold, I send you out lambs among wolves. Carry no money bag, no sack, no sandals; and greet no one along the way. Into whatever house you enter, first say, 'Peace to this household. If a peaceful person lives there, your peace will rest on him; but if not, it will return to you. Stay in the same house and eat and drink what is offered to you, for the laborer deserves his payment. Do not move about from one house to another. Whatever town you enter and they welcome you, eat what is set before you, cure the sick in it and say to them, 'The kingdom of God is at hand for you. Whatever town you enter and they do not receive you, go out into the streets and say, the dust of your town that clings to our feet, even that we shake off against you. Yet know this: the kingdom of God is at hand. I tell you, it will be more tolerable for Sodom on that day than for that town."

Today, Jesus Teaches Us to Use Our Time to Be True Disciples

I have coached youth sports for many years; years that far exceeded my own son's participation in these programs. Through all these years, when asking others to volunteer their time to help with our town's sports programs, I hear a common objection. It isn't a lack of sports knowledge or even coaching experience. The most common objection is "I don't have the time." Some even go further, making assumptions about their schedule compared to mine, saying: "You have the time, I don't."

The reality is, I do not "have" the time. I own my own business; am a partner in two other ongoing organizations; serve on my Church's Pastoral Council, Facilitate Adult Bible Study… the list goes on. You get the idea. I'm not patting myself on the back, I'm just making a point: I do not "have" the time to take on this additional role—I MAKE the time.

One reason I make the time is that there is a need. When Jesus talked about the harvest being abundant but the laborers being few, He was expressing how great the need is, to spread the good news of the Gospel.

MAKE the Time to Spread the Word

So today despite what your schedule looks like, regardless of how busy you think you are, you need to be charitable with your time by making some of it available to spread the Word and help bring in the harvest.

Your "setting out" can be a text or email. A phone call would be better. A personal visit or conversation would be best. Make the time and see how many people you can tell about Jesus' love. You may want to share a favorite piece of scripture or a personal story about how Jesus has or is changing your life. With a heart full of charity, today, MAKE the time to help the Father with the harvest.

Personal Journal

How much time did you make today for this part of your walk? Five minutes? Fifteen minutes? An hour? Was it enough? Could you have given more time?

Who did you share the Good News with?

How did you communicate: text, email, phone, in person? Was that the best option?

How did you feel?

_____
_____
_____
_____
_____
_____

Can you see yourself doing this often?

_____
_____
_____
_____
_____
_____

A Step Further: Sharing Today's Walk

Today is another day where "sharing" is built into the task, but try this: After you think you have shared with everyone you can, find one more! That "one more" could be the person most in need!

Day 15

FURTHER ALONG: CHARITY/TALENT

Luke 6:30
Give to everyone who asks of you, and from the one who takes what is yours do not demand it back.

Today, Jesus Teaches Us to Give Unselfishly

Near the climax of the movie "Field of Dreams," Ray Kinsella, played by Kevin Costner, reaches his boiling point. In response to a mysterious voice, he has built a baseball field in the middle of his cornfield and welcomed ghostly, former major leaguers to come and play. His actions expose him to ridicule and possible financial ruin. Yet he isn't getting anything back while others may benefit.

"I haven't once asked what's in it for me," he shouts at the ghost of baseball great Shoeless Joe Jackson.

Jackson replies, "What are you saying, Ray?"
"I'm saying... what's in it for me?" he replies sheepishly.
"Is that why you did this—for you?"

Sure, Ray wants something, some reward. It's natural. It's human.

When we use our talents we often lose focus. Slowly the effort shifts from the surface goal—raise money... help someone in need... feed the hungry... tend to the sick—to something more focused on ourselves. We slip into doing things for our own glory, acknowledgement, position, advancement. We give our talent, but hope—even if it is just subconsciously—for some acknowledgement of our efforts.

Many times we give to others that ask for something and *do* "demand it back," in the form of appreciation, prestige or reward.

Give, Acknowledging Others and the Lord
Today you will give of your talent—it can even be a continuation of the walk started on Day 5, or another talent you didn't circle on your original talents list—but you will give UNSELFISHLY.

Now here's the challenge: If credit is offered, refuse it.
Respond to appreciation with appreciation for another's role in the project:
"... No, thank *you* for listening (or watching, or participating)"
And ultimately—"Don't thank me, thank the Lord for allowing me to help"

Change your focus from yourself to others and the Lord.

This skill is a mindset. You may use your talent today, but the opportunity to not ask for anything in return may not come up immediately. You need to set your mind and be ready. Practice it at the next opportunity—and often.

Acknowledge others. Acknowledge the Lord. Start today.

Personal Journal

What talent did you choose to use or continue using?

Did you find redirecting credit to others difficult?

Did you find redirecting credit to the Lord difficult, or did it feel right?

Do you think you can apply this principle every day?

What can you remind yourself of that will help you apply this principle?

A Step Further: Sharing Today's Walk

Sharing is inherent in today's walk, so the number of people reached is not limited. But stay focused on the idea: to share without expecting anything back and by your example glorify the Lord.

Day 16

FURTHER ALONG: CHARITY/TREASURE

Mathew 6:1-4
"[But] take care not to perform righteous deeds in order that people may see them; otherwise, you will have no recompense from your heavenly Father. When you give alms, do not blow a trumpet before you, as the hypocrites do in the synagogues and in the streets to win the praise of others. Amen, I say to you, they have received their reward. But when you give alms, do not let your left hand know what your right is doing, that your almsgiving may be secret. And your Father who sees in secret will repay you.

Today, Jesus Teaches Us to Give without Thanks or Pride

It feels good to give. It truly does. When we charitably share our treasure with a worthy organization or an individual in need, we often feel happy, fulfilled, satisfied. But why? Where does this good feeling come from? If we were to be completely frank—even painfully honest—that good feeling sometimes comes not only because we may have helped someone, but because we have raised our own stature. We improved our standing in the church, in the community, among our co-workers, friends and family. *I raised more money. I gave more. I am a shining example that everyone should follow—but no too closely: I want to stay #1.* These are pretty common motivations and honest responses when given the opportunity to share your treasure.

Today we have a challenge that is both simple and complex. Follow Jesus' instruction: Do not give for others to see. If others seeing your charity is your reward, won here on earth, then there is nothing the Father need do for you in heaven. Give without fanfare. Give without hope for thanks or attention. At the same time—and here is the complex part—give, without dwelling on the act yourself: "Do not let your left hand know what the right hand is doing."

Practice Charitable Amnesia

Today begin a habit of giving and forgetting about it. Think of it as *Charitable Amnesia*: Giving and not patting yourself on the back. Giving and not dwelling on the good feeling. Do not be your own judge of your good and righteous acts. Do it because you know it is right to do and then move on—to the next good thing you can do. Although your next planned charitable donation may be days or weeks off, let's not miss the opportunity to put this into practice today. Make a contribution—a healthy one (remember the poor widow's example from day 6) and then forget it. Put it out of your mind. Looking for the approval undermines your act and patting yourself on the back is a waste of time. There is more work to do. There are other tasks at hand. Move on.

Personal Journal

There is no personal Journal today. If you followed direction, you acted and moved on. You should not be thinking or writing about it. Pray that your mind shifts focus to other tasks for the Lord.

Day 17

FURTHER ALONG: SCRIPTURE

John 8:31-32
Jesus then said to those Jews who believed in him, *"If you remain in my word, you will truly be my disciples, and you will know the truth, and the truth will set you free."*

Today, Jesus Teaches Us to Continue in His Word

"If you remain in my word, you will truly be my disciples…"
So today, I ask you this: How can you **remain** in his Word if you do not **know** his Word. Sure, like a broken clock that is right twice a day you may find yourself in accordance with his Word here and there, now and again, but you will not be able to "continue" in his Word if you do not know it, understand it and put it into practice. This book in itself is a beginning. You are reading Jesus' words, contemplating them and through a variety of exercises putting

them into practice and making them part of your very being. At the end of 30 days, at the end of this first of many Walks with Jesus, if you have approached this prayerfully and with an open heart you will have His guidance and His instruction to carry you forward. But don't assume the devil is not at work and the distractions of daily life won't derail you. You need vigilance and commitment to follow through.

Start by Learning His Word
Today you will learn his Word—so you can act on it, put it into practice—*continue in it*. There are literally hundreds of bible study courses. There are in-person studies you can attend. There are books and online courses. But for now, let's approach this simply. Pick a gospel: Mathew, Mark, Luke or John. Read it today. Note what touches your heart in your Personal Journal below: A moment that inspires you; A phrase that moves you. There's no minimum or maximum number. When you are done, ask yourself why those particular chapters, verses or phrases touched you. Again, note your answers in your Personal Journal.

Now, pick one and see if you can act on it. In other parts of this walk we have given you specific actions to take related to specific verses. This is more of your free choice, a free elective: From the gospel that you read, what one thing would you like to act on today—don't worry if it repeats something else we've done or might do on this journey. The point is, His Word touched your heart, the Holy Spirit moved you, and you must act on it, today! Now. While the passion is there, even if it is just an ember, let's see if we can fan it into a flame.

Are you motivated to give to the poor like the widow in Mark 12:43-44? Are you inspired to pray? Are you moved to make a commitment to not judge others? It doesn't matter. Your "moved" heart is Him speaking to you. Act on His Word and truly be one of His disciples. Continue in His Word by committing to an ongoing plan to read, discover and do... To Do More!

Personal Journal

List scripture entries and why they inspired you. Use additional paper, if needed.

_____

_____

_____

_____

_____

_____

How can you act on one or more of these?

_____

_____

_____

_____

_____

A Step Further: Sharing Today's Walk

Once you have acted, see if the story of today's walk can inspire others to join you or go down their own scripture-inspired path.

Day 18

FURTHER ALONG: EVANGELIZING / SHARING THE WORD

Mark 5:19
But he would not permit him but told him instead, *"Go home to your family and announce to them all that the Lord in his pity has done for you."*

Today, Jesus Teaches Us to Share the Word

It is our responsibility as Christians to share the Word; Jesus clearly tells us so in the verse above. Sharing the Word with the intention of introducing people to God's Love and thereby converting them is evangelization. Can there be a greater gift you can bring to someone?

It, however, can be one of the most intimidating things imaginable. For many of us, it can be the ultimate act of putting ourselves out there. Putting ourselves on the line—the firing line. Will we be looked down on as crazy? Naïve? A Jesus freak or Bible thumper? Will the people we speak to become uncomfortable and start avoiding us?

Moreover, can we speak on Jesus' behalf? Will we know the right things to say?

Any of these concerns are normally big enough to stop us dead in our tracks.

Let me ask you this: did you ever have an exciting secret that you just felt as if you were going to explode if you didn't tell someone? That's how I see telling people about Jesus: a big, wonderful secret, too good to keep to yourself. And, when you think about it, that's all evangelizing really is: Telling people about Jesus. It's not always telling people what Jesus can do for them—although what he can do is plentiful—it can simply be telling them about what Jesus has done for you.

There's no need to go in armed for bear. No need to be prepared to carry on every form of biblical debate or win an argument. Jesus can do that on his own, quite well, thank you. What He's asking you to do is simply plant the seed.

He's already armed you with what you need to start: your own stories of how he has touched your life. We all have those stories to tell: If you recognize his many blessings, you have those stories to tell. If you are new to Christianity or just don't think you have been blessed, perhaps you need to clear away the clouds and think about your blessings. Do you have a family, people you cherish? Friends? A place to call home? A job? Have you been offered the opportunity to help others? Do you enjoy nature? Are you alive? Perhaps, holding this volume in your hands and having the chance to share it is your blessing.

Tell Others What Jesus Has Done for You
On Day 8 you focused on sharing His Word with one person. Today, you need to think about casting a wider net. List any groups you are part of. These might be formal groups such as clubs, business groups, or civic organizations. Or, they may be informal groups such as friends from the local bar or the

gym. Commit that the next time you meet, you WILL bring up how Jesus has blessed you. You don't have to orchestrate a discussion. It doesn't have to be an extensive testimony. Just share your blessings and how you feel thankful to your Savior Jesus Christ. See what happens. You may be shocked, as I have been many times when just by getting the ball rolling, others began to share. Or, you may need to have faith, that while no one else may have shared—at that moment—that what you said was a seed—a seed that got them thinking.

Personal Journal
Pre-task entries:

Making the list is easy, do you think you will have the courage to follow through when your group meets? Why or why not?

_____

_____

_____

_____

What benefits do you expects from this task?

_____

_____

_____

_____

Post-task entries:

Did you have the courage to follow through when your group met? Why or why not?

_____
_____
_____

Describe your experience:

_____
_____
_____

What benefits did you see from this task?

_____
_____
_____

A Step Further: Sharing Today's Walk

Today's task is about sharing... just remember there is no limit to how many times or how often you do this: Doing so should become part of who you are.

Day 19

FURTHER ALONG: LOVE THY NEIGHBOR

Luke 10:30-37

Jesus replied, "A man fell victim to robbers as he went down from Jerusalem to Jericho. They stripped and beat him and went off leaving him half-dead. A priest happened to be going down that road, but when he saw him, he passed by on the opposite side. Likewise a Levite came to the place, and when he saw him, he passed by on the opposite side. But a Samaritan traveler who came upon him was moved with compassion at the sight. He approached the victim, poured oil and wine over his wounds and bandaged them. Then he lifted him up on his own animal, took him to an inn and cared for him. The next day he took out two silver coins and gave them to the innkeeper with the instruction, 'Take care of him. If you spend more than what I have given you, I shall repay you on my way back.' Which of these three, in your opinion, was neighbor to the robbers' victim?" He answered, "The one who treated him with mercy." Jesus said to him, "Go and do likewise."

Today, Jesus Teaches Us to Truly Understand Who Our Neighbors Are

I heard the story of the Good Samaritan for years and did not fully understand it. I must have been well into my 40's before someone explained the relationship between Samaritans and Jews that is central to the story. To explain it as concisely as possible, Jews and Samaritans were at odds, on opposite sides, enemies. So the fact that a Samaritan should care for the robbed and beaten Jew was not just a case of one person caring for another. It was one adversary caring for another. Finally, the power of the story was clear to me. One failing in modern religion is that too often, those who teach and preach assume the congregation understands all the nuances of the verse or parable. But let's try to put this in both context and perspective for us. The congregation, in an attempt to understand the commandment, asked Jesus "who is my neighbor." By the parable Jesus defines your neighbor as anyone you come in contact with, but especially those in need.

Treating "Non-Friends" Sympathetically
On Day 9 of this journey, we tried to get to know one or more neighbors better so we could understand their needs and thereby Love them. Today our opportunity is twofold and then some. Think about that person from Day 9. Have you learned enough? Can you do for them, even if it just extending a hand of friendship? I hope so. If not, we need to work on that.

Now, for today: you will make a new list in your Personal Journal. I truly hope you don't have those you consider enemies, but perhaps there are those you don't always see eye-to-eye with. Perhaps you flat out just don't get along. List these people. Don't worry about the issues between you and them. Instead, next to each name, note what you know of them: Their likes and dislikes; pastimes; needs.

Now, ask yourself: How can you treat them sympathetically? How can you help them? Write down your thoughts.

_____

_____

_____

_____

_____

Next, choose one person and one action, from what I hope is a short list, and ACT!
Be the Good Samaritan.
Love thy neighbor, who you are not friends with, by treating this person with caring, sympathetic action.

Personal Journal

THOSE I DON'T SEE EYE-TO-EYE WITH	WHAT I KNOW OF THEM	HOW I CAN TREAT THEM SYMPATHETICALLY

A Step Further: Sharing Today's Walk

Do you know someone who is not seeing eye-to-eye with someone else? List them below.

_____

_____

_____

_____

_____

Will sharing today's walk inspire them to make a change?

_____

_____

_____

_____

_____

Day 20

FURTHER ALONG: FOLLOWING THE LORD

Mark 12:29-30
Jesus replied, *"The first is this: 'Hear, O Israel! The Lord our God is Lord alone! You shall love the Lord your God with all your heart, with all your soul, with all your mind, and with all your strength.'"*

Jesus Teaches Us to Follow Him with All Our Soul, Mind and Strength

Do we love the Lord, our God, with everything we have? We like to think so. It's a given, right? If you think you know God, you love Him, even when you are faced with challenges large and small. I, however, would venture a guess that VERY few of us really follow this fully. Re-read the words in their totality, to their literal extreme: *"You shall love the Lord your God with all your heart, with all your soul, with all your mind, and with all your strength."*

That means with everything you have, everything you are and everything you ever will be. That kind of love takes effort. More effort than we have ever put into any report, earning any promotion, charming any lover, winning any championship or beating any disease or foe.

How can we focus our hearts, minds, soul and strength on this one goal: to Love God?

On Day 10 Martha hurried about, worried about the wrong things and missed the point, while Mary spent time with Jesus. We asked you to put Jesus at the top of your To Do list. Today, we need to add zeal and passion to that effort. Passion that must become full and totally consuming. God is not a hobby you can drop when you lose interest or when day-to-day things distract you. He is all that matters.

Approach Jesus with Joy, Anticipation & Excitement

Today you must spend time with Jesus but realize who he is and the opportunity you have—salvation and eternal life. So… Pray with Joy. Attend Church eagerly. Meditate in anticipation… share with excitement and joy.

Jesus is great and the ability to know this is the greatest of blessings. Today, as a start, pick one thing you do to spend time with Jesus and approach it with a different mindset—with joy! Or with a different physical tact—perhaps you pray alone—invite someone to join you. Do you spend time with Jesus by giving to the poor? Tell someone you meet—with a smile on your face—that this is what you do[4] and invite them to join you. Let's get on our feet and follow Jesus with Joy today! You can't leave anything on the table – you must give it your all.

---

4 *You may perceive a subtle conflict between sharing what you do and Mathew 6:1—3 which tells us to give in secret. The difference is in the motivation. If you are announcing the good things you do to collect esteem, honors and rewards, then that is a problem. If you are sharing your actions to increase the affect for the Glory of the Lord, then you are on the right track. Be careful. This can be a slippery slope. Remember: for His glory, not yours*

Personal Journal

Did you pray differently? Attend Mass differently? Explain.

After spending time with Jesus did you call a friend or relative to share the excitement?

_____

_____

_____

_____

_____

_____

_____

_____

_____

If you had trouble finding the passion, fear not. Pray and try again. He Loves you.

A Step Further: Sharing Today's Walk
Sharing Today's Walk can be an extension of your passion—it all depends on how you approach it. Think about it.

DAYS 21-30

*Jesus Teaches Us
What We Need
For the Rest of the Way*

Day 21

FOR THE REST OF THE WAY: PRAYER

Mathew 6:33
But seek first the kingdom [of God] and his righteousness, and all these things will be given you besides.

Today, Jesus Teaches Us to Pray to Attain the Kingdom of God

There are innumerable things we can pray for: health, wealth, safety for ourselves and our family members, happiness for our children, success in our careers. There is nothing wrong with praying for what you believe you need. But often we pray for earthly things. Even good health, while not materialistic, is temporary. As is world peace since this world itself is temporary. I don't want you to take anything out of your prayers or for you to think there is anything wrong with praying for your immediate needs. There isn't. They can be beautiful things and how gratified we are and how much is our faith increased when we see these prayers answered. But, what I do want you to do is add something to your prayers.

Pray for the Most Important Thing
Today, and from this day forward, follow Jesus' instruction and pray for higher things. Seek the Kingdom of God, and his righteousness. Pray that you are right with God. Pray for the Grace of light as St. Ignatius of Loyola instructed in his Examen—the ability to see yourself as God sees you. Pray that every action of every day keeps you on the path to the Kingdom of God. Seek higher things and you, in his time, will be rewarded more than you can imagine.

A common approach to prayer involves 4 steps:
1. Pay homage—Giving Him all honor and glory
2. Demonstrate penitence—Confess your sins and seek forgiveness
3. Give thanks for all your blessings
4. Supplication—Present your needs

Starting today, add to those needs the Kingdom of God!

Reminder: One way to pray is through a simple conversation with Jesus. Start by returning to the prayer place you selected on the first day of this journey. The place that hopefully you have visited every day since we started. Breathe. Clear your mind. Then open your heart for a relaxed conversation with Jesus. Tell him about your day, not just your list of grievances and your needs... these can be a part of your prayer, but why not open your heart to Jesus' presence.

Speak with Him as you would speak to a friend:
- » "Here's what I did today, Lord..."
- » "I enjoyed the sunrise you created..."
- » "I saw dogs playing in the park..."
- » "I'm praying that this or that will work out for my son..."
- » "Jesus, I'm hoping I am right with you, and if not, that I can find the strength so I can be with you someday in Your Kingdom in Heaven..."

He's always there and is ready to listen.

Personal Journal
Was today's approach new for you?

_____
_____
_____
_____

If it was, how did you feel about it?

_____
_____
_____
_____

If it was not new, how can you increase your focus on the Kingdom of God?

_____
_____
_____
_____

A Step Further: Sharing Today's Walk
Sharing is an excellent way to increase, not only, your focus on the Kingdom of God, but the perspective of the person you are sharing with!

Day 22

FOR THE REST OF THE WAY: FORGIVENESS

Luke 6:32-35

For if you love those who love you, what credit is that to you? Even sinners love those who love them. And if you do good to those who do good to you, what credit is that to you? Even sinners do the same. If you lend money to those from whom you expect repayment, what credit [is] that to you? Even sinners lend to sinners, and get back the same amount. But rather, love your enemies and do good to them, and lend expecting nothing back; then your reward will be great and you will be children of the Most High, for He Himself is kind to the ungrateful and the wicked.

Today, Jesus Teaches Us to Love Our Enemies

On Day 2 of this walk we asked you to forgive those who you felt trespassed against you by making a list and then, one by one, letting go, in your heart, of that grievance.

On Day 12, Jesus asked you to be a peacemaker. We focused that idea and asked you to reach out to one person, close to home, who you had a disagreement with. Perhaps you were at a stalemate with this person or were holding a grudge. We suggested you take the first step. Hopefully you were able to do that. And if that situation still hasn't resolved, remember things are handled in God's time, not ours. Stay the course and remember to pray about it.

Today, brings what may be more of a challenge for many: The idea of loving your enemies.

It is hard to imagine loving someone if you hold a grudge, are angry or can't let go of the trespass that has put you on opposite sides. You are not being asked to agree with your enemy, but to forgive them and then you can love them. You can love a family member or a close friend even after a disagreement. But how much more are you imitating Christ by forgiving and opening the door to loving your "enemy."

Make the Commitment
As on Day 2, you may want to start with a list. This time, however, you are making the commitment to love this person—or these people—despite their politics, moral values or actions that have put you on different sides of the fence. Focus on the person or persons. Try to separate the person from their actions. Release any negative thoughts. Commit to love them as they are children of God and recognize that judgement lies with Him alone. Add them to your prayers. The change of heart will shine through in your actions.

However strong the differences, you must love your enemies.
Why? Reread Jesus' words: *"then your reward will be great and you will be children of the Most High."*

If you don't think you can meet this challenge, ask for help: **Pray to Jesus for the strength to be like him!**

Personal Journal
List the people you will commit to love, despite all differences.

_____

_____

_____

_____

_____

_____

Questions:
Did you doubt your ability to meet this challenge when you first read it?

_____

_____

_____

_____

_____

_____

Did the exercise of making another list make it easier? Describe your experience overall.

Did the chance to be a son of the Most High soften your heart?

A Step Further: Sharing Today's Walk
If you are successful with today's walk I would imagine you couldn't help but want to share it: "You'll never believe what I did..."
But, be careful. If you are loving your enemies don't share the story to show how great you are, share it to inspire others. Share it to glorify the transformative power of Jesus' instruction.

Day 23

FOR THE REST OF THE WAY: HELPING OTHERS

Luke 5:31-32
Jesus said to them in reply, *"Those who are healthy do not need a physician, but the sick do. I have not come to call the righteous to repentance but sinners."*

Today, Jesus Teaches Us to Help Those Most in Need

On Day 3 we looked close to home, asking you to help a family member or friend with a task or problem. On Day 13 we cast a wider net looking to help as many people as possible by sharing a favorite piece of scripture and talking about why that verse spoke to your heart.

Today, you will look to those **most in need and give them your help** by advising, encouraging and motivating them. Jesus says *"Those who are healthy do not need a physician, but the sick do. I have not come to call the righteous to repentance but sinners."*

Help Them, Starting Today

Do you know someone who is sorely in need of changing their ways—a real hardcase? Someone who is deeply in need of spiritual guidance, or someone whose actions could lead to trouble in this world or the next? Perhaps you know someone who is abusing their body with drugs or alcohol, but have been hesitant to say anything. Perhaps you know someone who has fallen in with "the wrong crowd." And if those around you are so blessed that you feel they may not fit today's description, remember that there are plenty of people, such as at-risk youths in local programs, who might benefit from your insight and encouragement. There are ways to reach out to these people. There are community centers or even prisons that may have programs where your volunteerism could make a difference for someone.

Whoever the individual or whatever the group, you must commit to help them, starting today.

There are a least two challenges in this part of your walk. One, you may have to summon some courage to reach out to this audience. After all, they are the ones most likely to not only resist your helping hand, but strongly resent it. Two, even if you make positive inroads, it may be some time before what you do actually bears fruit. That means your first impression might be feeling that you failed. Give it time. What you say today may take time to produce a positive affect. Even if you are chased away, the seed of your words may bear fruit in the future.

In fact, patience is critical to this part of your walk. It may well take more than a day to even figure out who needs such help. Just start the ball rolling today. If that's all you can do, take heart and persevere.

Personal Journal

Were you able to think of someone right away or did it take some contemplation?

Was the person close to you or a complete stranger?

Did today's path take a great deal of courage? Explain.

Can you continue this effort with the same person based on his or her needs?

_____

_____

_____

_____

If you volunteered to help a stranger through an organization, might this ministry become part of your life, going forward?

_____

_____

_____

_____

A Step Further: Sharing Today's Walk

Be careful: If you helped someone, sharing the story might risk exposing information that is private or confidential. Sharing should always involve talking to God about what happened and how you felt. In cases of privacy, you may need to stop here.

If, however, what you do is more on an organizational or institutional level like working with a prison group, you may be able to reach out to others a bit more. Remember, the more you share, again maintaining all required privacy of any individuals, the more help you might get in working this mission. That's when we all win: The helpers, as well as those helped!

Day 24

FOR THE REST OF THE WAY: CHARITY/TIME

John 3:16
For God so loved the world that he gave his only Son, so that everyone who believes in him might not perish but might have eternal life.

Today, Jesus Teaches Us to Give Our Time... for the Rest of Our Time

Other than our loved ones, it can be said that the most precious thing we have is Time. On Day 4 we charitably allotted some of our time to help someone with a simple need or task. On Day 14 we contributed more time, MAKING the time to help the Father by sharing the Word and helping him with the harvest.

As incomprehensible as is the Father's sacrifice of Love for us—giving his only Son—we need to look to it as an example, every day.

Commit Our Time

Let us take our own precious time—and, while it does not compare to the Father's gift—let us do our best to exemplify his Love by committing a fair piece of that time for an extended period.

Today, will be a day when you broaden your horizons and add a new ministry! You are reading this for a reason. Maybe that reason is discovering a new purpose.[5]

Go to a blank screen or piece of paper.
What ministry, in or out of the church, can you commit to on an ongoing basis?
- » Can you commit time every week at a soup kitchen?
- » A youth program or prison program?
- » Can you teach a second language?
- » Volunteer at a Hospital?
- » Teach someone to read?
- » Spend time visiting a retirement home—particularly seeing someone you may not know, who doesn't have anyone to visit them?

Can you charitably give your time—over time—to your church or in your community?

Make your list. Narrow it down. Set your goal of how much time you will offer up and for how long. Reach out to whoever you may need to talk with to get the ball rolling.

Become a living example of giving. Could it be for a month? God Bless you! A year? Praise the Lord! For the rest of your life? Now, we're talking!

---

[5] This task applies even if you are already the posterchild for volunteerism, spending vast amounts of time helping. Don't worry. You can do more. You will MAKE the time—He will help you. Just ask.

Personal Journal

Was it difficult to make your list? Or, did you have too many and needed to narrow your list?

_____

_____

_____

_____

Did you have trouble making a final choice?

_____

_____

_____

_____

A Step Further: Sharing Today's Walk

You will naturally tell others about your new ministry, but when you do, make sure you tell them why you took this on.

Day 25

FOR THE REST OF THE WAY: CHARITY/TALENT

Mathew 5:16
Just so, your light must shine before others, that they may see your good deeds and glorify your heavenly Father.

Today, Jesus Teaches Us to Give of Our Talent to Glorify the Lord

It crossed my mind that this scripture seems to conflict with another: Matthew 6:1-4 which instructs us to do things in private, because if we are rewarded here on earth by men, there is no reward in heaven from the Father. It also can be seen to conflict with Day 15 where we tried to focus on giving of our talents selflessly—without hope of reward. But be careful. Jesus is not saying let your light so shine before men that they may see your good works *for your elevation and praise.* He is saying let your light shine so they may see your good works—not you. And, the purpose of shining the light on those good works is to glorify your Father.

So let's tie this together:
1. We all have talents—they should not be buried, but used for the glory of the Father (see Day 5)

2. We should not ask anything back—your talents are God given. Acknowledge others and most importantly acknowledge the Lord (see Day 15)

3. Today you will shed light on your works—not yourself—and draw a very strong connection from the use of your talent to God who gave you that talent. You will do this to inspire others to do the same. That is, to use their talents to glorify the Lord.

Make Sure People Know it was The Lord
Now we need to go back. Look at how you have used your talent—anytime in your life. Is there a way to go back and acknowledge the Lord? Can you add a dedication or acknowledgment to something you wrote? Can you call other participants in a project and discuss how you were all blessed to participate—get their minds refocused on the Lord. Can you acknowledge the Lord's role in your good works on Social Media... with real examples? If you feel you took too much credit or may have lost focus, honestly admit that and refocus on Him.

Today, you will ensure that the Lord is glorified in what you have done in the past and you will commit to always acknowledging him in the future *"...that they may see your good deeds and glorify your heavenly Father."*

Personal Journal

Were you embarrassed by either the thought or admission that you had taken credit for works made possible only by the talents He had given you?

Did you feel relieved or right with God once you acknowledged others and Him?

Can you make this your life pattern going forward?

A Step Further: Share your action with others

The nature of today's task requires some degree of interaction with others, but don't mistake that for all the sharing that is possible. Share today's walk with someone not involved in the works you are acknowledging His role in. This will increase the likelihood that the "outside" person you are sharing with will be inspired on their own to do likewise in their own life.

Day 26

FOR THE REST OF THE WAY: CHARITY/TREASURE

Mark 10:17-25

As he was setting out on a journey, a man ran up, knelt down before him, and asked him, "Good teacher, what must I do to inherit eternal life?" Jesus answered him, *"Why do you call me good? No one is good but God alone. You know the commandments: 'You shall not kill; you shall not commit adultery; you shall not steal; you shall not bear false witness; you shall not defraud; honor your father and your mother.'"* He replied and said to him, "Teacher, all of these I have observed from my youth." Jesus, looking at him, loved him and said to him, *"You are lacking in one thing. Go, sell what you have, and give to [the] poor and you will have treasure in heaven; then come, follow me."* At that statement his face fell, and he went away sad, for he had many possessions.

Jesus looked around and said to his disciples, *"How hard it is for those who have wealth to enter the kingdom of God!"* The disciples were amazed at his words. So Jesus again said to them in reply, *"Children, how hard it is to enter the kingdom of God! It is easier for a camel to pass through [the] eye of [a] needle than for one who is rich to enter the kingdom of God."*

Today, Jesus Teaches Us to Give From Now On

"…his face fell" …I think almost all of us have some empathy for this man. He wanted to inherit eternal life—as we all do—but the price Jesus puts before him in terms of the cost in this world seems high "for he had many possessions". One of the reasons the price may seem high is its relationship to time. Giving up everything you have here and now for the future—even if the payoff is eternal life with Jesus—seems hard until the idea of eternal life with Jesus stops being just words and is accepted for what it truly is.

But, are we really supposed to give up everything? Are we supposed to leave ourselves with nothing, becoming poor and destitute? No, but what we are being asked is to commit to following Christ and to place our commitment to him above all earthly things, all earthly possessions: to value nothing above the Lord and be willing to demonstrate that through our actions.

Commit to a Lifetime of Charity

On Day 6 you learned to give a little more than usual. On Day 16 you were asked to do so privately—without fanfare, without expecting a pat on the back and without even dwelling on it yourself.

The job is not done.

There are many in need—yes the poor will always be with us (Deuteronomy 15:11)—but what can you do here and now to ease their burden? Giving, being charitable, truly giving of your treasure is not a one-time thing. One time eases your conscious. Today you need to commit to a lifetime of charity.

Where can you commit your effort—in one place or more than one—for a lifetime of giving of your earthly possessions, following Jesus without hesitation?
- » Can you give more to your church monthly?
- » To a scholarship fund for the underprivileged annually?
- » A national charity, regularly?
- » Can you start your own non-profit foundation?

This is a big challenge. For many in our material world, this may be the biggest challenge. But, what do you have to lose? Just your place with Jesus, eternally. Listen to what he says: "...take up your cross and follow me." (Mark 8:34)

Personal Journal

Was it easy to come up with one or more organizations to give to on a regular basis?

_____

_____

_____

_____

Did you think of an individual or a family, rather than an organization that needed help? Explain.

_____

_____

_____

_____

Did you pray before making your final decision?

_____

_____

_____

_____

_____

A Step Further: Sharing Today's Walk
Sharing can inspire others and give you more hands making lighter work, or it can motivate them to seek their own path. Either way, God is glorified by your actions... so... ACT!

Day 27

FOR THE REST OF THE WAY: SCRIPTURE

Mark 8:35
For whoever wishes to save his life will lose it, but whoever loses his life for my sake and that of the gospel will save it.

Today, Jesus Teaches Us to Commit Fully to Scripture

If we look at the context of the scripture above, Jesus has just told his disciples he must be turned over to his enemies, suffer and die. Peter encourages resistance. Jesus' responds strongly: "At this he turned around and, looking at his disciples, rebuked Peter and said, *"Get behind me, Satan. You are thinking not as God does, but as human beings do."* He summoned the crowd with his disciples and said to them, *"Whoever wishes to come after me must deny himself, take up his cross, and follow me. For whoever wishes to save his life will lose it, but whoever loses his life for my sake and that of the gospel will save it. What profit is there for one to gain the whole world and forfeit his life? What could one give in exchange for his life? Whoever is ashamed of me and of my words in this faithless and sinful generation, the Son of Man will be ashamed of when he comes in his Father's glory with the holy angels."* (Mark 8:33-38)

The direction on our path is clear. Losing your life is about letting go. Literally, letting go of your physical life if that is what is required, but also letting go of what you **thought** was important and embracing what **is** important. It is about following Him instead of current trends or what society tells us is important. In letting go of those things, we let go of our lives - laying all these things down and following Jesus. To do so is to open yourself to doubt, derision, insult and even injury as He did on Calvary Hill. This is what it means to take up your cross.

So today your path takes you toward a more complete commitment to losing your life for Jesus' sake and the Gospels. On Day 7 of this journey, you took a leap of faith into the Bible, making notes on select, possibly random, readings. On day 17 we acknowledged the availability of many Bible Study options, but on that day we focused on working independently, working on a single Gospel and developing our Personal Journal regarding what touched us, and then sharing it.

Group Bible Study: Do It and Share
Today, let's return to the idea of group Bible Study and commit to two things:

1. Find and participate in a group Bible Study. Some last just a few sessions, others require more of a commitment

2. Spread the word about what you are doing

In selecting a course, remember there are existing studies or you could start your own group study, even if just within your own family at first.
- » Of existing courses, there are online ones or in-person studies you can attend, either through a church or independently.
- » In terms of starting your own group, remember you can rely on materials readily available at bookstores or online.

Think about what would work best for you.

If you do decide to start your own group don't worry about the number of people. Remember, Matthew 18:20: *"For where two or three are gathered together in my name, there am I in the midst of them."*

In spreading the word there are many ways to do this. You can casually bring it up in conversation, emails, texts or social media posts. This part is not necessary to organize and recruit more people. It is simply to let it be known what you are doing for His glory, not yours. You are offering an example that others might follow: you are planting seeds. Remember Mark 8:38: *"Whoever is ashamed of me and of my words in this faithless and sinful generation, the Son of Man will be ashamed of when he comes in his Father's glory with the holy angels."*

Personal Journal
Did you find today's path particularly challenging? If so, why?

What do you think you could do to make yourself more comfortable in embracing this task?

_____

_____

_____

_____

Is committing to Bible Study something you could continue for life? Why or why not?

_____

_____

_____

_____

A Step Further: Sharing Today's Walk

Sharing earlier, rather than later, will help build your group study or could turn your individual initiative into a group! Give it a chance.

Day 28

FOR THE REST OF THE WAY: SHARING THE WORD

Luke 4:42-43

At daybreak, Jesus left and went to a deserted place. The crowds went looking for him, and when they came to him, they tried to prevent him from leaving them. But he said to them, *"To the other towns also I must proclaim the good news of the kingdom of God, because for this purpose I have been sent."*

Today, Jesus Teaches Us to Spread the Word Far and Wide

True disciples follow Christ. To truly follow him we must imitate him.

Jesus says: *"I must proclaim the good news of the kingdom of God, because for this purpose I have been sent."* Then this is our purpose as well.

On Day 8 we evangelized by reaching out to one person. On Day 18 we went further, committing to reach a group. Now we must follow Jesus and his mission, today and from now on.

But how can we tell people—beyond our own current circle of relatives, friends, and business acquaintances—the good news of the kingdom of God? How can you share His Word and what He has done in your life? And, like Jesus, once we have delivered the message there, how do we continue to "other towns"?

If contemporary communication is possible, work with your list of friends and send an email, publish an article, a post or tweet. Whatever method of communication you use, broadcast your message the best you can. Start today.

For some of us it may be better to go old school—literally and figuratively. Think of those you went to school with. Make a list. Who are you still in touch with? Who could you reconnect with?

Write them a good old-fashioned letter.

Create a Dialogue
On Days 8 and 18 we took a gentle approach to sharing the Word and evangelization: Bearing witness to the impact Jesus was having in our lives. I like that approach: as if Jesus is saying "Just tell them what I have done."

But today, let's go further with our message as well—let's insist on more of a dialogue: After sharing the Word and telling your story of how Jesus has affected you, encourage each person you touch to share their own story— with you and with others beyond their own circles.

You may be surprised at what happens once you start the ball rolling.

If they are truly lost and don't see their own story—or truly have no story yet—then thank God for the opportunity to help. Talk to them and see if you can help them see how God truly has affected them. Sometimes it is just a matter of perspective. Light their fire, set them on their own mission. Bring them to Jesus.

While it may seem out of the norm for you, it can happen. But it can only happen if you start. Please, do it. Do it today.

Personal Journal
What were your feelings about today's task before you started?

_____

_____

_____

_____

What surprised you most in the results?

_____

_____

_____

_____

A Step Further: Sharing Today's Walk
Sharing the Word on a wider scale need not stop. In fact, it must never stop... keep the ball rolling!

Day 29

FOR THE REST OF THE WAY: LOVE THY NEIGHBOR

Matthew 25:34-40

Then the king will say to those on the right, 'Come, you who are blessed by my Father. Inherit the kingdom prepared for you from the foundation of the world. For I was hungry and you gave me food, I was thirsty and you gave me drink, a stranger and you welcomed me, naked and you clothed me, ill and you cared for me, in prison and you visited me.' Then the righteous will answer him and say, 'Lord, when did we see you hungry and feed you, or thirsty and give you drink? When did we see you a stranger and welcome you, or naked and clothe you? When did we see you ill or in prison, and visit you?' And the king will say to them in reply, 'Amen, I say to you, whatever you did for one of these least brothers of mine, you did for me.

Today, Jesus Teaches Us to Love Our Neighbor Unceasingly

I have often said being a Christian is not an easy task. In fact, it is very difficult—at least to try and do so on our own. Being a Christian with His help is much easier. Today we are challenged to do something that can only be done with His help: With His support—which you must ask for through prayer—and through his constant intercession. We just don't have the strength to do it otherwise. So let's do it with him. Here it is…

On Day 9 you had to learn more about a single neighbor so you could love him or her. On Day 19 you had to Love a neighbor that you did not necessarily see eye-to-eye with. In both cases, if those people were in need you had to give them sympathetic care.

Today Jesus asks you to provide sympathetic care not once, but EVERY time. Wow! What a challenge! But remember: It is doable with him. He is there walking at your side.

Re-read today's scripture.

Not that feeding the hungry, visiting those in prison, tending the sick or taking in strangers one time isn't noble, but you cannot care and then arbitrarily stop caring. It is not an item on a checklist to be marked off as "Done." As long as you have compassion, energy and the practical strength to do so, there are neighbors to be cared for and ours is the responsibility to do so.

Pray for Guidance—And Act

The reality is our time, energy and resources are limited. So today, pray for guidance. Ask where to focus your energies and when you have your direction, follow it. Wholly. Aggressively. Joyfully. And when the battle is getting the better of you, raise up yet another of your unending prayers and ask for His guidance and more strength. Listen with your heart and do as much as you can for those in need. Love Thy Neighbor… Because helping and loving them is the same as loving their Father—Your Father.

Personal Journal

As you read today's task, where did you initially think you might want to focus your energies?

_____

_____

_____

Did you pray about it? Was anything different revealed by the Father through your prayers?

_____

_____

_____

Are you excited about what direction you might be lead in? Why or why not?

_____

_____

_____

A Step Further: Sharing Today's Walk

Sharing your thoughts with a friend, family member or advisor might help you find your direction. Once you have it, be sure to share where Jesus has led you.

Day 30

FOR THE REST OF THE WAY: FOLLOWING THE LORD

Luke 6:46
"Why do you call me, 'Lord, Lord,' but not do what I command?

Today, Jesus Teaches Us to Follow the Lord in All that We Do

When Jesus spoke to me, I did not see this day.
I did not see the day I would write for Him the last of these 30 "walks".
But as I wrote, over time I would look forward to this last entry and wondered how He would guide my hand:

- » "What will He have me do?"
- » "What earth-shattering, game-changing direction would Jesus give me to pass on to you?

» "What chapter or verse would He point me too?"
» "Would He give me a new, up to now unrevealed meaning to convey?"

What I find—what He has pointed me to—is not something new, but more importantly it is whole and all encompassing: *"Why do you call me, 'Lord, Lord,' but not do what I command?"*

So, the final step on this 30-day walk shows we have looped back to the beginning and the rest of your unending journey has the same wisdom running through it all: Do what he commands.

All of what He had me tell you for 30 days, you are to do.

All of this and more. All of what is in the Gospels—His Words—are to be followed.

Oh what a hard task that might seem, but not really.
Go forward:
» Trying with all your heart, mind, soul and strength.
» Trying deep in prayer.
» Trying with all your time, talent and treasure.
» Trying with all your energy.
» Rely on the Bible. Love your neighbor and spread the Word.
» Try by Loving him.

And, if you stumbled on your walk, missed, or didn't do your best with one of these 30 tasks, try again. He'll give you a hand. He hasn't given up on you and He doesn't want you to give up on you either.

Personal Journal

Do you feel overwhelmed by this last task? If so, what might help you gather strength?

_____

_____

_____

_____

_____

_____

_____

_____

_____

_____

A Step Further: Sharing Today's Walk

At this point if you have been sharing your journey with others, there is no need to stop. If you have not been sharing, now is a wonderful time to start.

WHERE DO YOU GO FROM HERE? DAYS 31–40!

First, by now I pray you see that none of us ever walk alone, and while it is easy to get lost, you have the greatest guide ever to help you out.

From here, let's see if this journey is really fulfilled: Over the next 10 days revisit these 30 walks.

Using your Personal Journal will help.

Consider if there are any tasks you missed, could have done better with, or enjoyed enough to repeat.

Pray and let Him be your guide.

Hopefully I have been a good and faithful disciple and through me, He has given you new paths that you can travel every day—with Him—throughout eternity.

God Bless.

ACKNOWLEDGEMENTS

First and foremost...
To God the Father almighty creator of heaven and earth, God the Son, our Savior Jesus Christ and God the Holy Spirit who dwells in all of us: With him, nothing is impossible.

Special Thanks To:
- Elizabeth Rector, who didn't have to go it alone and keep us all together, but did anyway. Thanks for the Christmases, Mom.

- Edward Rector, who volunteered and did what he did under fire, thereby reminding me that I never really have anything to complain about.

- Dennis Rector, who started by giving me baseball and 40+ years later reminded me who I am.

- Gerry Gartner, there since the 7th grade.

- Father Paul A. Cannariato, whose clear direction helped me to the finish line of this book—practically and spiritually.

- » Annette (Gandolfi) Perine, who took this book for its first "test drive" and whose responses convinced me to push forward.

- » Tara Mayberry, whose publishing professionalism helped carry this book to the finish line.

- » Marianne & Joe Reilly, Andrea & Lane Abernathy, Gerry Gartner, Dennis Rector, and Susan Rector for the leg-up when I needed one.

- » Eileen Greer, because sometimes knowing there's a friend a phone call away is enough.

- » Mike Bender, my *Brother from another Mother.*

- » Jim Psihas for the wild ride that provided the breathing room and confidence to wrap this up.

- » Ralph Barrientos for sharing his faith without equivocation.

- » Maik Walther who always reminded my "no risk, no fun."

- » TobyMac and Brennan Manning who inspire us to "Speak Life."

- » John Wayne who taught me most of the rest, but especially not to burn daylight.

- » And finally, to *Team Rector* for all the Love and Support.

ABOUT THE AUTHOR

Dave Rector
Dave is a disciple of Jesus Christ, a husband, father, youth baseball coach, Pastoral Council member and Bible Study Ministry leader. A successful entrepreneur, he has served both start-up companies and some of the world's leading organizations as a consultant, marketing strategist, writer, video producer and creative director.

A prolific writer, Dave has worked in virtually every format from marketing, feature articles, and general fiction to children's fiction and spiritual literature. Dave has been honored with more than 70 national and international business awards for writing, production, and creative excellence. He has held board positions in church and sports organizations, not-for-profit and for-profit companies.

Follow Me: A 30-Day Walk with Jesus is his first book, now in its second edition. Dave is available for virtual and in-person speaking engagements and personal coaching.

For more information visit www.WordSparkMedia.com.

www.ingramcontent.com/pod-product-compliance
Lightning Source LLC
Chambersburg PA
CBHW040508110526
44587CB00046B/4301